How To Tell Your Personal Story: The Essential Guide To Memorable Storytelling

I0479089

Part three of **The Storytelling Mastery**: *How To Elevate Your Business and Build Personal Influence with The Power Of Storytelling*

Obehi Ewanfoh

© 2023 Obehi Ewanfoh
The Storytelling Mastery
Aclasses.org/books

ISBN: 9798385975044
info@obehiewanfoh.com
Obehiewanfoh.com

What I have learned from over 10 years of storytelling experience, 2013 to 2023

Table of Contents

DEDICATION

To my beloved father, Ewanfoh Ohenbhen,

I dedicate this book to you with all my heart. You left us when I was just a little child in primary two, and I have missed you every day since then.

I wish you could have been there to see us grow up and share all our experiences with us. But even though you are no longer with us, your memory, and the lessons you taught us continue to inspire and guide me every day.

This book, "How To Tell Your Personal Story: The Essential Guide To Memorable Storytelling," is my tribute to you and your legacy. It's a guide for anyone who wants to tell their own story, whether it's to a small group of friends, in business environment or to a large audience.

I hope this book will serve as a lasting tribute to your kind and gentle soul, which will always remain in our hearts.

Rest in peace, dear father. You will never be forgotten.

With love and gratitude,

Your son,

Obehi.

IMPORTANT:

This book series is designed for those looking to elevate their businesses and build personal influence with the power of storytelling.

This is not just another book about storytelling. This is a **Full Package** to help you start from the ABC of storytelling to some of the most advanced strategies of leveraging the power of story in your business.

Start your 7 days free access to our Storytelling Mastery Academy.AClasses.org

INTRODUCTION

Everyone has a story to tell. Whether it's a tale of triumph, a journey of self-discovery, or a moment of heartbreak, your personal story holds the power to connect and inspire others.

But how do you take your experiences and craft them into a compelling narrative that will captivate your audience? That is at the core of what sets you apart and you should never underestimate that awesome power irrespective of what you do.

With this step-by-step instruction and practical tips, you will learn the secrets of turning your unique story into a memorable masterpiece. This is what this book, "How To Tell Your Personal Story: The Essential Guide to Memorable Storytelling" is here to help you achieve.

From identifying the themes that drive your narrative, to developing characters and building tension, you will discover the right tools you need to captivate and engage your listeners. In case this is your first book in "**The Storytelling Mastery**", I encourage you to read the previous books because they set the foundation for this very one.

Whether you are looking to share your story with the world or just want to be a better storyteller in your personal life, this guide will give you the confidence and skills you need to bring your stories to life.

The art of storytelling is not just about entertaining others with your experiences, it's also a powerful tool for self-expression and self-discovery. If you are an African diaspora, you should pay attention to that. And if you are a content creator or a small business owner, you should equally pay attention to that.

Now, there is another thing to put at the back of your mind. As you delve deeper into the art of storytelling, you will not only learn how to craft captivating stories, but you will also gain a deeper understanding of yourself and your own life experiences. And that is something to be taken seriously.

In these pages, you will find exercises designed to help you uncover the themes, characters, and conflicts that define your personal story. You will also discover techniques for bringing your stories to life through vivid descriptions, dialogue, and pacing in a way to perfectly takes your audience along.

The following is a short clip from Akash Karia's book, TED Talks Storytelling: 23 Storytelling Techniques from the Best TED Talks. I think you should give it serious consideration.

"People are hardwired to listen to stories. Stories are the way human knowledge was passed down before the written word. Storytelling is hardwired into our brains. It's the natural way that our brains learn and process information."[1]

Akash Karia is a peak performance coach who has trained over 180,000 people worldwide, from bankers in Hong Kong to senior executives in Thailand to government members in Dubai and much more. You might want to consider reading the book, TED Talks Storytelling: 23 Storytelling Techniques from the Best TED Talks.

Now, whether you are a seasoned storyteller or just starting out, 'How To Tell Your Personal Story' will help you tap into the power of your own life experiences and share them with the world. So, let's get started and discover the storyteller within you.

How the book series is set up

It was in the early period of 2013 that I first started to collect data about the African diaspora community and then, it was mainly those in northern Italy

---

[1] *TED Talks Storytelling: 23 Storytelling Techniques from the Best TED Talks by Akash Karia.*

through a series of interviews. It was an interesting encounter with the direct protagonists, many of whom have now relocated to different parts of the world in their immigration journey.

I have already published two books from the research project, (*The Journey: Africans In Verona* and *The Color Of Our Children*), now, 10 years later, I still love what I have done, documenting the experiences of the people so that those who will be here later can benefit from it. Feeling that some other persons might also be interested in taping into the power of stories, I have decided to share what I have learned about the art of storytelling all these years.

But is it important for more members of the African diaspora community to learn about storytelling? Well, I leave you to reflect on that.

The book, drawn from my research experience of working with different people over the years, it's voluminous, and knowing the feeling of some people towards reading in the community, I have decided to break up the work into manageable chunks for easier consumption. And for those who want to read the full story in one book, that is also available.

Your storytelling guides

The storytelling guides are designed to help you get more out of this reading. Each chapter of the book starts with a premise of what you can get by the end of the reading. That is followed by diving into the specific topic, citing instances, and elaborating on the chosen argument for further clarification.

Towards the end of each chapter are "your storytelling guides", a set of actionable recommendations on how to leverage what was discussed in the specific chapter. If you pay attention to this section of the book, you will have a lot to benefit from it as designed.

Your chapter takeaways

Let me be clear that this book is not just to be read for the pure purpose of wasting away your time. There is a clear thought behind every chapter that is included in this book series, otherwise, that chapter should not have been there. So, from each chapter, there are key takeaways for you.

Just after the "storytelling guides", you will see some highlights which are in line with the initial premise at the beginning of the specific chapter. This is to be sure that you get the true value for which that particular chapter of the book was written. That is not by accident, so pay attention.

CHAPTER 1: GETTING STARTED

Storytelling is an art, and like any art, it takes practice to master. Learn how to get started with storytelling and make it work for your business.

Master the art of storytelling by understanding the basic concepts and principles, and start experimenting with different techniques to find the perfect way to tell your story.

I want us to start this chapter with a quote from Robert Lowell Moore Jr., author of The Green Berets, The French Connection, and several other books:

> *"Inside each of us is a natural-born storyteller, waiting to be released."*[2]

Perhaps you haven't thought of yourself as a natural-born storyteller and that is why you haven't

---

[2] *Robert Lowell Moore Jr.*

released your storytelling potential so you can leave your mark on the world. I really mean that. You too can have your mark, a dent in this world if you understand the power of storytelling. But the question is "are you ready to do that?"

Welcome back to the third book on "**The Storytelling Mastery**". My intention here is to help you understand how to leverage your storytelling skills so you can earn more as a content creator and small business owner.

Up until this stage in the book series, we have considered different tips and strategies about the basics of storytelling and what you need to know to have a good footing in your storytelling adventure.

That was important because nobody does any serious thing without first considering the basics. In this chapter of the book, you will learn how to start your storytelling, how to get started, and the importance of your personal story. Now, let's jump to the conversation on how to get started with storytelling.

How to get started with storytelling

There are different ways to get started with storytelling. It can be anything from writing short stories, novels, and plays to creating short videos or film scripts.

Before there were methods, styles, textbooks, and discussion plans, there was storytelling. Good storytelling has always been the known form of communication and telling a good story can be considered the earliest form of teaching and passing on knowledge and vital information in human society.

A good story, therefore, can be said to fulfill the following conditions for a people:

- Entertainment purpose,
- Educational purpose,
- And the purpose of enlightening.

With storytelling, the most important thing is to keep your audience engaged and interested in your story.

Now, imagine what you can do with that as a content creator and digital entrepreneur with lots of people coming to consume your content. That is a huge opportunity.

Everyone has a story to share and there are lots of ways to start doing just that. Creative writing classes, creative writing exercises, and creative writing workshops are all effective ways for people to develop the skills they need to write creatively.

If you are serious about storytelling, you don't need to sit there and start looking at a blank space, not knowing what to put on the paper. I truly do believe that everyone has a story to share, and you can start with yourself. Let's talk more about that. There is no better place to start your storytelling than yourself.

Start your storytelling with yourself

I recently came across a quote somewhere that reads:

> *"The ability to see our lives as stories and share those stories with others is at the core of what it means to be human."*[3]

That is so true… And I know that it's not always easy to "create your story" but a good place to start can be by writing the story of your life. Here are 3 effective ways to write a personal story that will engage with your readers:

---

[3] *John Capecci and Timothy Cage - Goodreads.com*

➢ *Start at the beginning and with a goal in mind*

Starting at the beginning makes a personal story seem more interesting and engaging to the listener because this makes them feel that they know the whole story. It's also a good idea to start by telling the reader what your goal is.

For example, you want to find out how people feel about alcohol, so you will write about your experience with drinking alcohol excessively. This can be how you started and how it ended with a lesson for your audience to take away. I am not saying you must have been an alcoholic at a point to write an alcohol-related story. That was an example and I hope you get the point.

Here are examples of 6 people who started a storytelling career, using their personal stories. I am sharing this story with you so you can learn from them:

1. **Brené Brown**: Brené Brown is a research professor and author who gained popularity for her TED Talk on vulnerability. She tells personal stories about her struggles with shame, perfectionism, and vulnerability, and how these experiences have shaped her life.
2. **Chimamanda Ngozi Adichie**: Chimamanda Ngozi Adichie is a Nigerian novelist and

storyteller who often draws from her own experiences growing up in Nigeria. Her work explores themes of identity, culture, and gender, and she has become known for her ability to create complex nuanced characters.

3. **Trevor Noah**: Trevor Noah is a comedian and talk show host who grew up in South Africa during apartheid. He has written a memoir, "Born a Crime," which tells the story of his childhood and the challenges he faced growing up as a mixed-race child in a racially divided society.

4. **Glennon Doyle**: Glennon Doyle is an author and activist who writes about her personal struggles with addiction, eating disorders, and marriage. She has been praised for her honest, raw storytelling and her ability to connect with readers on a deep emotional level.

5. **J.D. Vance**: J.D. Vance is an author and venture capitalist who grew up in a working-class family in rural Ohio. His memoir, "Hillbilly Elegy," tells the story of his upbringing and the challenges he faced as a member of the white working class in America.

Telling personal stories can be a powerful tool for connecting with others, building empathy, and creating understanding. When we share our own experiences, we invite others to see the world through our eyes and to feel what we have felt. This can help to break down barriers between people and build bridges of understanding and compassion.

Personal stories can also inspire and motivate others. When we share our struggles and how we overcame them, we can offer hope and encouragement to others who may be going through similar challenges. By sharing our successes and failures, we can also show that everyone is human and that it's okay to make mistakes and learn from them.

In addition, personal stories can be a way to preserve and celebrate our cultural heritage and identity. When we share stories of our ancestors and our cultural traditions, we help to keep those traditions alive and pass them on to future generations.

Overall, telling personal stories can be a powerful way to connect with others, share our experiences, and make a positive impact on the world around us.

➢ *Be personal and write about yourself*

Writing a story about the experiences that are important to you is an effective way to keep readers engaged. If you have strong opinions on an issue, then it is appropriate for you to discuss your opinion in your story.

If there are events or people in your life that are difficult for you, then this can be a time when you share what it was like for you and how things have gotten better.

To make sure your writing is personal, only talk about what matters to you, and don't write about anything else unless someone asks for it or unless it is important for the story you are telling.

Example of 5 popular authors who are personal in their writing. I recommend you study their works, so you can learn from them:

1. **Maya Angelou**: Maya Angelou was an American poet, memoirist, and civil rights activist who often wrote about her personal experiences as a black woman. Her memoir, "I Know Why the Caged Bird Sings," is a powerful account of her childhood and the challenges she faced growing up in the segregated South.
2. **David Sedaris**: David Sedaris is a humorist and essayist who often writes about his personal experiences in a witty and self-deprecating style. His work covers a wide range of topics, from his family to his travels to his struggles with addiction and mental health.
3. **Cheryl Strayed**: Cheryl Strayed is an author and essayist who is best known for her memoir, "Wild," which chronicles her solo

hike along the Pacific Crest Trail after the death of her mother. She often writes about her personal struggles and the transformative power of nature and self-discovery.

4. **Roxane Gay**: Roxane Gay is a writer and professor who often draws from her own experiences as a queer woman of color. Her work includes both fiction and nonfiction, and she is known for her honest and unflinching storytelling style.

5. **Elizabeth Gilbert**: Elizabeth Gilbert is an author and speaker who often writes about her personal experiences in a way that is both relatable and inspiring. Her work covers a wide range of topics, from creativity and spirituality to relationships and personal growth.

These are only some of the examples of popular authors who are personal in their writing. You can learn a lot by studying their work.

➢ *Use anecdotes in your stories*

Anecdotes are short stories that give readers a glimpse into your life before delving into more detail and providing an epilogue of sorts in which you reflect on what happened as a result of this event or experience.

To be more effective, anecdotes need to have the same three-part structure as stories: the background, the event, and the conclusion. It is essential to give details of what happened during the incident so that your readers can understand it properly and draw their own conclusions if needed.

The type of writer you are, and the story you want to tell, will determine how they work. You may prefer one method over another or use a combination of techniques, many of which I have shared with you in this 5-part book series, "**The Storytelling Mastery**".

Some writers like to get right into words, while others might organize their thoughts before sharing their finished product with the audience. You always want to see what works better for you. Now, there is a question, is it even important to tell your personal story? Well, that is a good question. Now, let's look at that shortly.

Make your story more memorable with the N.B.A technique

Crafting a memorable narrative fosters a profound bond with the audience. When professionals and entrepreneurs relate their personal encounters, challenges, and achievements, they establish a sense of trust and empathy, fostering robust relationships and inspiring customer loyalty. That is the important part of memorable storytelling, it helps build a strong connection with the audience.

To make your storytelling more memorable using the N.B.A. technique, consider the following strategies:

1. **Engaging Openings**: Begin your story with a captivating and attention-grabbing opening in the Now phase. Hook the audience with a compelling scene, intriguing question, or an impactful statement that immediately piques their curiosity and draws them into the narrative.
2. **Emotional Connection**: Focus on developing relatable characters with whom the audience can emotionally connect. Use the Before phase to explore their backgrounds, desires, and challenges, allowing the audience to form a strong bond with them. This emotional connection helps make the story more impactful and memorable.
3. **Unexpected Twists**: Incorporate surprises and unexpected twists throughout the story, particularly during transitions from one phase to another. These unexpected elements keep the audience engaged and on the edge of their seats, enhancing the memorability of the storytelling experience.
4. **Visual and Sensory Descriptions**: Use vivid descriptions and sensory details to create immersive imagery in the audience's minds.

Engage their senses by painting a vivid picture of the settings, characters, and events, making the story come alive and leaving a lasting impression.

5. **Thought-Provoking Endings**: Craft an ending in the After phase that leaves the audience with something to ponder or reflect upon. Provide closure to the narrative while leaving room for contemplation, allowing the story's themes or messages to resonate with the audience beyond the storytelling experience.

6. **Well-Structured Transitions**: Ensure that the transitions between the Now, Before, and After phases are seamless and well-crafted. Use hooks, cliffhangers, or intriguing revelations to smoothly transition from one phase to another, leaving the audience eager to know what comes next.

7. **Variety and Creativity**: Experiment with different storytelling techniques and narrative approaches within the N.B.A. structure. Incorporate elements such as humor, suspense, or poignant moments to add depth and variety to your storytelling, making it more memorable and engaging.

By incorporating these strategies, you can make your storytelling more memorable and impactful. The N.B.A. technique provides a solid framework, and these additional elements help enhance the emotional connection, engagement, and overall impression left on the audience.

You can learn more about the N.B.A. storytelling technique by checking out chapter 6 in (Storytelling Basics), book one of the 5-part storytelling series.

Why write your personal story

Telling your personal story is a powerful way to connect with others and build community within the African diaspora as much as in other communities. As you reflect on your journey and share your experiences, you will gain a deeper understanding of yourself, your cultural heritage, and your place in the world. Not only will you inspire others who may be facing similar struggles, but you will also leave a legacy that celebrates your unique contributions and experiences.

Writing your story is more than just documenting your past. It's a chance to process and heal from difficult experiences, and to grow as a person. By exploring the themes and patterns in your life, you will be able to identify opportunities for growth and positive change.

You might be thinking that you are not a great writer and therefore you shouldn't write or that no one will read your story. But that is not always the case. Write if you feel the fire burning inside of you. Write within your capacity and if really writing is your thing, you will soon grow your wings and fly with it like the pros.

In the words of Octavia Estelle Butler, an African-American science fiction author and a recipient of the Hugo and Nebula awards, "You don't start out writing good stuff. You start out writing crap and thinking it's good stuff, and then gradually you get better at it. That's why I say one of the most valuable traits is persistence."

You never want to underestimate Octavia E. Butler. Born on June 22, 1947, in Pasadena, California, Butler was raised by her widowed mother and she grew up to become a phenomena writer after practicing and practicing. After years of handwork unending, Butler became the first science-fiction writer to receive a MacArthur Fellowship in 1995. You too can get inspiration from her works and zoom the lens on your story.

Did your parents migrate to Europe from Africa for a reason they have told you several times? What about your own personal experience, growing up; your hopes and aspirations? You certainly must have a viewpoint about the world that people will miss if you do not share them. Do not think that is irrelevant because you surely are relevant.

Your story is an important piece of the larger puzzle, and by sharing it, you will contribute to the rich, diverse, and complex tapestry of the African diaspora community and humanity in general. Writing your story is a form of resistance against cultural erasure and amnesia, and a way of taking control of your narrative and ensuring that your voice is heard, especially in your business world. Never forget that.

Now, here are 5 reasons for using your personal stories in your business:

1. **Building connection with customers**: Sharing personal stories can help build a connection with customers by creating a sense of shared experience or relatability. Customers are more likely to trust and engage with businesses that feel authentic and human.
2. **Creating brand identity**: Personal stories can help create a brand identity that sets a business apart from competitors. By sharing unique experiences or perspectives, businesses can differentiate themselves and create a stronger emotional connection with customers.
3. **Demonstrating expertise**: Sharing personal stories can also demonstrate expertise and knowledge in a particular area. By sharing experiences or insights, businesses can establish themselves as experts and build credibility with customers.

4. **Engaging customers**: Personal stories can be a powerful way to engage customers and keep them interested in a business's products or services. By sharing stories that are entertaining, inspiring, or educational, businesses can create a more engaging and memorable experience for customers.
5. **Inspiring action**: Personal stories can also be a powerful tool for inspiring action or creating change. By sharing stories of personal growth or overcoming challenges, businesses can inspire customers to take action or make positive changes in their own lives. This can create a sense of purpose and mission for the business, beyond just making a profit.

As you will learn when you engage in writing and sharing your story, the process is a transformative and empowering experience. Not only will it help you understand and connect with yourself, but it will also help you connect with others, build community, and leave a lasting legacy that celebrates the rich and diverse experiences of the African diaspora.

The following is a clip from a masterclass publication:

> *"Whether you're a bestselling author working on your next book or a first-time writer whose goal is self-publishing, there are a few*

essential questions to ask yourself before beginning work on your book idea."[4]

Going further in the article, three fundamental questions were presented and you might need to consider them when starting your writing:

- "Do you have the time and mental energy to commit to writing a whole book?"
- "Are you prepared to develop potentially unfamiliar skills, like self-editing and rewriting?"
- "Do you have a basic grasp of your main characters, plot, or subject matter?"

Now, let me share my personal experience with you about "**The Storytelling Mastery**". How do you think the book came to be?

After the research and the request from different people like you who told me they wanted to learn about storytelling, I did not simply jump to my computer and start writing this book.

I first thought of the work, and how it should be transformational for people from not knowing much about storytelling to be able to create their own

---

[4] *How to Write a Book: Complete Step-by-Step Guide - Masterclass.com.*

stories. To do that I needed to ask myself, what I would need to know about storytelling and how I would approach it if I were new to the topic of storytelling.

The points I wrote down in the process, or if you like, the outlines became the building blocks of this entire book series. And I am sure that you can do the same for any type of story you want to write. That is how I wrote most of my books.

Of course, you are not me and you don't need to do it my way. And you certainly don't need to be afraid to experiment with different voices, styles, and story structures when writing. Want to learn more about story structure, consider checking out the previous book in the series, Storytelling Basics: How To Get Started In Telling Impactful Stories.

As long as you are willing to put in the time and practice, based on the ideas and techniques in this book, you certainly can create great stories for your audience and benefit from your creativity.

Let me repeat this. Do what comes easiest for you and walk your way up in your storytelling adventure. Keep the parts that work for you and disregard the rest until you have figured out everything for yourself.

Storytelling Guide – Getting started

Here are 7 things to consider when writing the story of your life:

1. **Purpose**: What is the purpose of your life story? What do you want to communicate to others? Having a clear purpose will help you stay focused and ensure that your story is meaningful and relevant.
2. **Audience**: Who is your audience? Consider who you want to reach and what they may be interested in hearing about your life. This will help you tailor your story to your audience and engage better with them.
3. **Life Themes**: What are the overarching themes in your life? Consider what experiences or events have shaped who you are and what you want to communicate to others.
4. **Honest Reflection**: Be honest with yourself when reflecting on your life. Consider both the positive and negative experiences and how they have shaped you. Authenticity is key to creating a compelling story.
5. **Perspective**: How do you want to present your life story? Will you present it chronologically or focus on specific themes or experiences? Choose a perspective that will

engage your audience and keep them interested in what you have to say.

6. **Storytelling Techniques**: Use storytelling techniques, such as descriptive language and rich dialogue, to bring your story to life and engage your audience.

7. **Emotional Resonance**: Make sure your story has emotional resonance with your audience. Connect with their emotions and tap into their universal experiences to create a lasting impact.

By using this technique, we can gain insight into our personal experiences and create a power story that our audience will easily relate to.

Your Takeaway From chapter one

Storytelling has become an essential tool for connecting with customers and creating a lasting impression. It can be a powerful way to evoke emotion, create engagement, and convey important messages in an impactful way. This is always relevant whether you are a small business owner who wants to elevate your brand or a content creator who needs better engagement with your audience.

Storytelling can be an incredibly powerful tool to boost your marketing efforts. This chapter of the book helped you understand how starting with your personal experience can help you create stories that are both captivating and compelling. Learn how to make the most of your storytelling to improve engagement with your target audience.

And talking of connecting with the African diaspora, telling your life story is a great way to foster stronger bonds with the people. As you reflect on yourself and become more open with those around you, you will gain a deeper understanding of who you truly are.

In the next chapter, we will talk about how to know your personal story and explore it deeper. Get ready for that.

CHAPTER 2: KNOWING YOUR PERSONAL STORY

Knowing your personal story is the key to understanding your brand's story. Learn how to uncover the unique and compelling story of yourself and your business.

Learn the art of storytelling by understanding your background experiences, and values, and use that as a foundation to create stories that truly resonate with your audience.

Let me begin this discussion by reminding you that, you really cannot serve others until you can first serve yourself. And how you want to serve is up to you to decide.

Welcome back to "How To Tell Your Personal Story", the third in "**The Storytelling Mastery**". That this book concentrates on you as the storyteller is intentional and this is what we are here for.

The techniques and different strategies you have learned about storytelling up until this time are only to improve your skills to become a better storyteller.

Yes, a better storyteller, but who are you in the midst of all these? What is your story and why do you have that kind of story?

Explore your personal story

This is the catch and I want you to think about it: You cannot change the past, but you have the chance to be here right now and you can shape the kind of future you want. It all starts with you and right now.

Do you know your personal story? Yes, I mean that because many of us do not. We simply live in a bubble, doing what we see others do, without being intentional about our lives and that is not good enough if we want to stand out from the noise around us. This is also why stories are important irrespective of what your purposes might be.

Now, here are five benefits of knowing your personal story in case you haven't given a serious thought by now. I encourage you to reflect on every single one of them:

1. **It helps you to understand yourself better**: By understanding your personal story, you can gain a greater insight into who you are,

your strengths, your weaknesses, and your motivations and desires.

2. **It helps you to make sense of your past**: Knowing your personal story can help you to make sense of your past experiences and how they have shaped you into the person you are today.

3. **It gives you a sense of purpose**: Another thing knowing your personal story can do for you is a sense of purpose and direction. It helps you see how your experiences and challenges have prepared you for the future.

4. **It can help you to overcome challenges**: By understanding your personal story, you can gain the insight and perspective needed to overcome challenges and adversity. If you think about it, these are never lacking in our lives.

5. **Understanding your personal story can help you connect with others**: Sharing your personal story with others can help you to connect better with them on a deeper level and build stronger relationships.

Always remember this: a personal story is a way of organizing the chaos of our past lives. It can be seen as a reflection of who we are and what we have experienced through life and how it has altered our worldview. Being able to capture your personal story will truly separate you from the crowd.

Yes, we are over 8 billion people in the world today but that should not take away your uniqueness because we are all unique and individual. We need this knowledge of uniqueness before we can be useful to our different groups and social stratifications.

Check out this short piece from John C. Maxwell, a New York Times bestselling author, coach, and speaker who has sold over 24 million books in 50 languages:

> *"For speakers, personal stories demonstrate your authenticity, they demonstrate your desire to connect. They demonstrate that you aren't afraid of being real, of standing up and showing your soul. They also show your humanity, with fierceness and frailties just like everyone else."*[5]

That quote is worthy of reflection, at least, in my view. Our stories can also be an alternative account of the events that occurred. They help us explore new perspectives or truths of the original events. Are you ready to embark on that journey? Because that might provoke some questions.

---

[5] *The Power Of Personal Stories - Johnmaxwellteam.com.*

You see, the little chick inside the egg will die if the egg does not break. That is the same for the seed you plant in the soil. So, a new life can only form after cracking the old one.

That is what we are talking about. And like Maya Angelou, the famous American poet, and civil rights activist once said, "There is no greater agony than bearing an untold story inside you." So, know yourself through deliberate self-discovery. Don't leave that to others to do for you.

Know where you are coming from

The popular saying has it that if you don't know where you are coming from, you most certainly do not know where you are going. I heard that adage several times and as a teenager who was very busy in the village, dipping hands into rabbit holes and sometimes jumping down from trees in the name of fun, I certainly took those words to heart.

I understand. We all have moments where we think about our childhood and how things may have impacted us. Though it is difficult to see into the past, it's important to reflect on your past experiences and try to better understand yourself.

To help you better evaluate yourself, here are some of the questions you could reflect upon. You really need to reflect upon them.:

- What kind of childhood did you have?
- Were you free to express yourself as a child?
- Did anybody take advantage of you?
- Did you suffer any abuse or bullies from other children?
- What kind of relationship did your parents have and how did that affect you?

Be sincere to yourself and provide honest answers to these questions because they are the key to better understanding your childhood and your past.

- How were you treated when you were at school?
- Were there any memorable incidents from your teenage years and your recent past?
- Is there any part of your past experience you feel strongly about, positively or negatively?

You could even take this further by keeping a record of your events and emotions. A good way to do this is by keeping a journal and writing down your thoughts.

Keeping a journal is an excellent way to maintain emotional stability so you can manage difficult situations through reflection.

Journaling will allow you to analyze your thoughts, emotions, and reactions. To track your performance and measure progress, try asking yourself why, for example, you were feeling sad at one point during the day. Learn as much as you can about your thinking patterns.

- What drives your thoughts?
- What makes you think positively or negatively?
- How are these thoughts linked to your past experiences?

By using this knowledge, you can fully understand yourself so you can better appreciate your present and build a better future ahead.

Kilroy J. Oldster is the author of Dead Toad Scrolls which was published in 2015. The book touches on narrating self-reflection, regarding the timeless questions of humanity: syncretic investigation of time, community, religion, nature, justice, and much more. Here is what she said about personal narrative:

> *"We must carefully cultivate the voice that speaks to us because an internal voice is the ultimate narrator of our charming and delightful personal story or the*

documentarian of our tragic and disgraceful plotlines."[6]

The stories we tell ourselves, according to Oldster become our functional reality, which format structures, the concourse of the nested emotional control panel that guides and girds us through the din of the present. You need to think about that for a moment.

Personal narrative writing is a way to combine all of your thoughts, memories, and beliefs into one story. Yes, you can redefine a better story for yourself. Let's look at some important parts of the puzzle, some limiting beliefs that might be working against you. Trust me, you will need to put them under control before you can progress.

Overcome your limiting beliefs

Let's be honest with ourselves, we are all incredibly hardwired to avoid "failure". Most people are ruled by the fear of failure and the feeling that they have to keep going at all costs just to avoid the backlash.

It might seem unbelievable, but when was the last time you gave up on something, and why? When

---

[6] *Kilroy J. Oldster – author of Dead Toad Scrolls.*

was the last time you tried something new or failed, and what did you tell yourself about it?

Born on October 7, 1931, and Died December 26, 2021, Desmond Mpilo Tutu was a South African Anglican bishop and theologian. He is best known for his work as an anti-apartheid and human rights activist. He was the Anglican Bishop of Johannesburg from 1985 to 1986 and then Archbishop of Cape Town from 1986 to 1996.

Now, this is one of Desmond Tutu's quotes that might keep you thinking:

> *"None of us comes into the world fully formed. We would not know how to think, or walk, or speak, or behave as human beings unless we learned it from other human beings. We need other human"*

I share this quote with you as a reminder that we are all human beings in need of one another. No one of us is born perfect. So, do not be ashamed to face your imperfections and limiting beliefs. It's perfectly fine to have those negative thoughts in our head, sometimes but what is not fine is to continuously live with them without challenging them.

Sometimes our brains can trick us into negative self-talk and believing things that are not true and this prevents us from achieving our full potential. This is known as a limiting belief, and you might have some that hold you back from the good things in your life.

There are many sets of limiting beliefs out there that hold people back from taking the right action in their lives. Some of your limiting beliefs could be as follows:

- I should avoid failure at all costs so that people don't laugh at me,
- I cannot start my own business,
- Money is the root of all evil, so I don't need it,
- I am not smart or talented like other people,
- I don't have enough experience or resources to pursue my passion.

These are only some of the thoughts most of us carry around in our minds and we are sometimes fully sure that they are right. But they are not, and you will need to find out for yourself. While it is possible it's not always easy to overcome these limiting beliefs you have accumulated over the years.

➢ *Examples of 7 popular people who overcame their limiting beliefs*

Think about them from the standpoint of how you can do the same. Countless people have overcome their limiting beliefs to achieve great things. Here are seven examples of popular figures who have done so:

Limiting beliefs are negative thoughts that we hold about ourselves and our abilities, which can prevent us from achieving our full potential. Overcoming limiting beliefs is an important step toward personal growth and success. Here are seven examples of popular people who overcame their limiting beliefs, along with tips on how others can do the same:

1. **Oprah Winfrey**: Oprah grew up in poverty and faced numerous challenges throughout her life, but she refused to let these obstacles hold her back. Instead, she used her experiences as motivation to succeed. One of her most famous quotes is, "The biggest adventure you can ever take is to live the life of your dreams." To overcome your own limiting beliefs, try adopting a similar mindset of determination and resilience.

2. **J.K. Rowling**: Before she became one of the most successful authors of all time, J.K. Rowling faced rejection from multiple publishers. She persisted in pursuing her passion, and eventually, Harry Potter became a global phenomenon. To overcome your own limiting beliefs, don't let rejection or setbacks discourage you from pursuing your goals.

3. **Elon Musk**: Elon Musk is known for his innovative ideas and bold ambitions, but he

has also faced his fair share of failures. For example, his first three rockets at SpaceX exploded. However, he didn't let these setbacks stop him from pursuing his dreams of space exploration. To overcome your own limiting beliefs, don't be afraid to take risks and learn from your mistakes.

4. **Michael Jordan**: Michael Jordan is widely considered to be one of the greatest basketball players of all time, but he didn't start out that way. He was actually cut from his high school basketball team as a sophomore. Instead of giving up, he used this setback as motivation to work harder and become better. To overcome your own limiting beliefs, remember that failure can be a powerful teacher.

5. **Serena Williams**: Serena Williams is one of the most successful tennis players of all time, but she's also faced criticism and discrimination throughout her career. However, she's always maintained a strong sense of self-belief and confidence. To overcome your own limiting beliefs, cultivate a positive self-image and focus on your strengths rather than your weaknesses.

6. **Steve Jobs**: Steve Jobs was known for his innovative ideas and relentless pursuit of perfection, but he also faced numerous failures and setbacks throughout his career. However, he always believed in his vision and never gave up. To overcome your own

limiting beliefs, stay true to your values and vision, even in the face of adversity.

7. **Malala Yousafzai**: Malala Yousafzai is a Pakistani activist for women's education and the youngest Nobel Prize laureate. She was shot by the Taliban at the age of 15 for speaking out about the importance of education for girls. Instead of letting this tragedy hold her back, she continued to fight for women's rights and education around the world. To overcome your own limiting beliefs, never give up on your convictions, no matter how difficult the journey may be.

These are just a few examples of the many people who have overcome their limiting beliefs to achieve greatness. Their stories serve as inspiration for anyone who is struggling to believe in themselves and their dreams. By adopting the mindset of these seven inspiring individuals, we can learn to overcome our own limiting beliefs and pursue our dreams with confidence and determination.

Like most people out there, you might be busy making excuses and giving yourself reasons to not take action, to not try something new. But do you know that there is so much you can do if you just get out of your comfort zone and follow your passions?

A common saying among my people, the Esan people of Nigeria is that "there is no point waiting if you have no one or something you are waiting for".

So, what are you waiting for? It's time to take the actions that can change your life instead of the same old excuses!

I understand that you need the courage to face the world and say something you can be held accountable for - your version of the truth and how you see the world. We all need that courage, and this is how Maya Angelou puts it:

> "Courage is the most important of all the virtues, because without courage you can't practice any other virtue consistently. You can practice any virtue erratically, but nothing consistently without courage."[7]

There are many ways to help yourself with limiting beliefs, like talking to a therapist and reading motivational quotes that can inspire you to take action.

Additionally, you can help yourself by understanding that it is just a belief. So, change the belief and adopt a new belief that can take you to your desired destination.

---

[7] *Maya Angelou – an American famous memoirist, poet, and civil rights activist.*

Negative self-talk can hold us back in a lot of different ways and it can make us feel like we don't deserve success, that we are not as good as others, and that the world is against us. It usually can manifest in the following ways:

- Self-sabotage and low self-esteem,
- Fears about our ability to succeed,
- Concerns about succeeding too greatly,
- And worries about the actions of others.

The first step in overcoming limiting beliefs is defining and identifying your beliefs. Write them down in a journal. keep track of your thoughts so you can understand what triggers those beliefs.

You can get more specific by examining different emotions like doubt, frustration, insecurity, and other types of situations that might be leading you to these thoughts.

Are you looking for strategies to overcome your limiting beliefs? Consider these 7 tips:

1. **Know your limiting beliefs**: The first step to overcoming your limiting beliefs is to know what they are. This may involve examining your thoughts and behaviors to see what patterns or negative beliefs are holding you back. Whatever it takes, just do it.

2. **Challenge the evidence**: Once you have identified your limiting beliefs, try to challenge the evidence that supports them. Are they true, or are they just assumptions or old stories that you are holding onto?
3. **Consider the pros and cons**: Understand the pros and cons of holding onto your limiting beliefs. Are they helping or hindering you in your life?
4. **Reframe your beliefs**: Once you have identified and challenged your limiting beliefs, try to reframe them in a more positive or empowering way.
5. **Practice self-compassion**: Be kind and compassionate towards yourself as you work to overcome your limiting beliefs. Remember that it is a process and that it is okay to make mistakes.
6. **Seek support**: Seek out the support of others, whether it be friends, family, or a therapist. Having someone to talk to and share your struggles with can be incredibly helpful.
7. **Take action**: Finally, take action to start living in a way that is consistent with your new, more empowering beliefs. This may involve setting goals and working towards them, or simply making small changes in your daily life. You need to take that action if you need the change.

It is after you have understood these, your limiting beliefs, and where you are coming from that you can successfully redefine your own story and truly embrace your journey.

This is fundamental, so let's consider one more way to finally get ourselves back from the grip of limiting beliefs. Trust me, you truly want to do this if you want to get the best out of your life.

Redefine your own story and embrace your journey

The story of your life is the one you create for yourself. It is about who you are and what you have done. It is about what makes you unique and special. And it is about the journey that has brought you to where you are today.

Erich Fromm is a German social psychologist. He was a German Jew who fled the Nazi regime to resettle in the United States. Here is one of his popular quotes about life's journey:

> "Let your mind start a journey thru a strange new world. Leave all thoughts of the world you knew before. Let your soul take you where you long to be...Close your eyes let

your spirit start to soar, and you'll live as you've never lived before."[8]

Can you close your eyes for a moment and feel what Erich is talking about? I think you should try that out.

Our stories are not always the same. Unlike some others, you may have had different kinds of difficulties in your past. Perhaps, you had a story of poverty, trauma, or suffering, but this should not hold you from progressing in life.

As I have already stated, you cannot change the past so, let it be. If anything in the process of redefining yourself, let your past work for you, not against you.

As well said in the book 'World Peace: The Voice of a Mountain Bird' by Amit Ray and Banani Ray,

> *"If you want to fly on the sky, you need to leave the earth. If you want to move forward, you need to let go the past that drags you down."*[9]

---

[8] *Erich Fromm - a German social psychologist.*

[9] *'World Peace: The Voice of a Mountain Bird' by Amit Ray and Banani Ray.*

That is a great piece of advice to remember. You see, it is impossible to change and remain the same. Don't get me wrong, I am not saying you should reject your story. No. you need to own your story. That is what I mean and that is what we have been talking about all along.

Owning your story is about taking responsibility, finding acceptance in yourself, and being able to be authentic. It's about knowing that you are enough and that it doesn't matter what others think of you because you are not supposed to be a pleaser to others.

You are a full human being on a mission and no other human being is exactly like you in this world.

Now, here are five ways to redefine your own story and embrace your journey:

1. **Reflect on your past experiences**: It will help to take some time to reflect on your past experiences and consider what you have learned and how you have grown as a result.
2. **Consider your values and priorities**: Think about what is most important to you and what you value most in life. This can help you to redefine your story and give it new meaning.
3. **Set new goals and intentions**: Set new goals and intentions for yourself and make a plan to work towards them. This can help you

to shape your future in a way that aligns with your values and priorities.

4. **Practice gratitude**: Consider practicing gratitude by focusing on the things in your life that you are thankful for. This can help you to shift your perspective and see your story in a more positive light.

5. **Share your story with others**: Sharing your story with others can be a powerful way to connect with them and gain new insights and perspectives. It can also help you to feel more connected and supported in your journey.

Do not be afraid to embrace your journey and the new you. Remember the words of William Ernest, in the poem, Invictus:

> *"I am the master of my fate. I am the captain of my soul."* [10]

Can you make that real in your case too? I think you should. And if you do, the door of possibilities will open for you when you know who you are and why you do what you do. At that point, nothing can stand in your way.

Yes, there will be some challenges and obstacles, but they will soon become your steppingstones

---

[10] *William Ernest - an English poet, writer, critic, and editor.*

because you know where you are going and your personal story should be shaped accordingly.

Storytelling guide - Knowing your personal story

Here are five steps to knowing your personal story. I have already shared some of them with you and are here repeated for their importance:

1. **Reflect on your past**: Take some time to reflect on your past experiences, both positive and negative. Think about the people, places, and events that have shaped who you are today.
2. **Identify key moments**: Do your best to identify the key moments in your life that have had a significant impact on you. These can be positive or negative experiences, but they should be moments that have shaped your beliefs, values, and understanding of the world.
3. **Understand your values and beliefs**: Reflect on your values and beliefs, and how they were shaped by your experiences. Understanding your personal values and beliefs will give you a better understanding of yourself and why you make the choices you make.
4. **Look at the patterns in your life**: Consider looking for patterns in your life experiences

and try to understand what they might mean. For example, do you notice a pattern of seeking out new experiences or a tendency to avoid certain situations?

5. **Share your story**: Share your story with others. Talking about your experiences with trusted friends or family members can help you gain new perspectives and deeper insights into yourself. This can also be a great opportunity to connect with others and create deeper relationships.

Those are good tips. By following them, you can gain a deeper understanding of yourself and your personal story. This knowledge can help you make sense of your experiences, understand your motivations, and make better decisions in the future.

Your takeaway from chapter two

This chapter of the book is incredibly important because it talks about you, the storyteller and I don't want you to ever underestimate that importance for any reason.

As a storyteller, you are important and it's intentional that this particular chapter of the book focuses on you. Sometimes, we are not different in what we do. I mean, our interpretations of events often shape the way we view ourselves and our future.

Knowing where we are coming from and being able to re-frame what we tell ourselves is essential to our well-being. Depending on the situation we find ourselves in, we need to find ways to change the story we tell ourselves so it can lead us toward more happiness in life.

Many of us do have limiting beliefs and this is not our fault sometimes. Therefore, we must learn to overcome our limiting beliefs, redefine our own story, and embrace our journey.

It will serve us well to accept that we do make mistakes and we should not be ashamed to admit that we have some difficulties. But moving past those challenges can make us feel much more in control of our lives. That is how we can shape a better and more intentional personal story.

CHAPTER 3: DEFINE YOUR STORYTELLING WHY

Storytelling is more than just sharing a story; it's about having a purpose. Define the why behind your storytelling and create a message that truly resonates with your audience.

Understand the problem you want to solve, the change you want to create, and the impact you want to make. Master the art of storytelling by defining the why and using it to create stories that are both meaningful and memorable.

I have a question for you. Why are you doing this? Do you have the answer to that? If your answer is no, then you need to pay more attention to this chapter of the book.

Welcome to chapter 3 of the book, How To Tell Your Personal Story: The Essential Guide To Memorable Storytelling. This is book three of "**The Storytelling Mastery**". Knowing how to define your storytelling "why" is a fundamental aspect of your storytelling adventure. Let's explore that.

The "why" is a powerful motivator and being able to find it is essential for a successful undertaking, any kind of undertaking, be it business on personal life. The "why" inside of you has the power to help you find your passion, purpose, and meaning. It will also help you determine how you want to live your life. Talking of life purpose, you might need to consider another of my book, "Discover Your Life's Purpose: How to Live with Passion and Energy". The book is available on amazon. So, give it a read.

Your "why" is what sets you apart from everyone else. It's the thing that has your purpose. It's what inspires you to take action. Your "why" is also one of the many things that inspire others to take action, spread your ideas, or buy your products.

The world is filled with all sorts of people. Everyone has a different purpose, and that's what makes the world so diverse and quite frankly, interesting to live in. Otherwise, living would have been boring and cumbersome.

While there might be more than 8 billion people in the world today, your 'why' is actually what makes you relevant, unique, and valuable, because you are standing for something specific, instead of just another human being in the world.

Now, here are some of the things to consider when defining your 'why':

- Remember what you enjoyed doing when you were a kid.
- Think back to the activities that allowed you to forget the passage of time and experience a feeling of pure contentment.
- What can help you give back to your community and at the same time get involved in the activities you truly enjoy?

Reviewing these will help you understand what you can define as the real purpose behind your storytelling and content creation.

You possibly came from a poor background and now your "why" is to help the children in your community access quality information and education. It's up to you to decide.

Define the why of your storytelling using the N.B.A. technique

Defining the "why" of your storytelling involves understanding the purpose, message, or intended impact of your story. Here's how you can define the "why" using the N.B.A. technique:

1. **Now**: Identify the central conflict or situation in the Now phase that serves as the driving force of your story. Ask yourself why this conflict is important to explore or why it matters to your audience. Consider the underlying themes, emotions, or social issues that the conflict represents.
2. **Before**: In the Before phase, delve into the backstory and motivations of your characters. Reflect on why their experiences, choices, or struggles contribute to the significance of the story. Consider the underlying values, moral dilemmas, or personal transformations that your characters represent.
3. **After**: Reflect on the resolutions, consequences, or outcomes of the story in the After phase. Ask yourself why these resolutions matter or what impact they have on the characters, relationships, or broader context. Consider the lessons, reflections, or messages that you want your audience to take away from the story.

By applying the N.B.A. technique, you can define the "why" of your storytelling more effectively. It allows you to understand the purpose behind your narrative, the relevance of the conflict, and the significance of the character's journey. Defining the "why" helps you create a more focused and impactful story that resonates with your audience and conveys a clear message or meaning.

Consider, checking out chapter 6 in (Storytelling Basics), book one of the 5-part storytelling series if you want to learn more about the N.B.A. storytelling technique.

Know what your values are

In the book "Find Your Why," Simon Sinek and his co-authors explain that a WHY Statement is both a reason for your friends to love you and what motivates you professionally.

Of course, you don't always need a professional why; instead, focus on personal why for your wins to be most sustainable. And because every other person out there is also a human being, they will find your story resonating with them.

The following is a clip from an interesting article on psychology today:

> "Life presents an endless series of decisions, large and small, that require you to make difficult choices. While many factors are involved, the critical factor in deciding may be your core values. These values tell you what kind of person you are, or want to

be, and provide guidelines, or even imperatives, for your actions."[11]

If I were you, I would reflect on that. At the end of the day, your values are important. Never forget that. They provide boundaries and guidelines for how you should live and work. So, you use them to measure and gauge your happiness and engagement with life at a macro level.

Now, here are five reasons why it is important to know your true values:

1. **Your values guide your decisions**: Knowing your values serves as a guiding light for your decisions and actions. It helps you to determine what is most important to you and what you should prioritize.
2. **Your values shape your identity**: Your values are a big part of who you are and what makes you unique, so understanding your values can help you to better understand yourself and your identity.
3. **Your values influence your relationships**: Your values can also shape your relationships and how you interact with

---

[11] *6 Ways to Discover and Choose Your Core Values: Knowing your values can guide your actions and give you inner peace. - Psychologytoday.com.*

others. Knowing your values can help you to form deeper and more meaningful connections with others.

4. **Your values help you to live a more fulfilling life**: By living in alignment with your values, you can live a more fulfilling and purposeful life. Pursue your passions and goals in a way that is authentic and meaningful to you.

5. **Your values can help you to overcome challenges**: Another thing knowing your values helps you do is to overcome challenges and adversity, as they can give you the strength and motivation to persevere and stay true to yourself.

If you think about it, it is you that people are connecting to not just your business. So, are you who say you are wherever you are? What I mean is this:

- What do you represent?
- What is your true value?
- Does your audience know this?

When I got to Italy in August of 2004, I met with different kinds of challenges. I remember being told on my very first day in Italy that I would go to jail because of what those I came to meet thought I would do. Sure, I saw what they were doing, and I even accompanied some of them to the street at one point, but when I saw what was going on, I left them on the street and returned home. And that was although I had no money and no possibility of working legally in the country.

That is not because I was better than the other Nigerians, I came to meet in Italy but because of my values and what I could be prepared to pay a price for. It was never about going to jail or being held accountable for my actions, but how does the action relate to and align with my core values as a human being? Never forget that.

Are you living your values by the decisions you make, the tasks you perform, and the products you sell? Your key values need to be reflected in the things around you.

The point, in the end, is that when the things you do, are a part of yourself, and how you behave matches your values, life will generally be of a higher level. You are satisfied and fulfilled.

When these don't match up with your values, that is when it can feel wrong. It can be a huge source of unhappiness for most people who suffer from this problem. So, know your key values and operate by them in everything you do.

It is important to know what motivates you and what helps you to do your best work. What motivates you could be personal or professional while being creative at work will allow you to do your best work. So, this is a call to know yourself inside out.

Create your "why" statement

To keep reminding yourself of your 'why', you might need to create your Why Statement and put it in a place where you can easily see it.

A Why Statement is a sentence that clearly expresses your distinctive contribution and impact. The concept was brought to life by Simon Sinek in his famous TED talk, "Start with why", which provides interesting insight into making your ideas more tangible.

If you haven't seen the video, I encourage you to see it on YouTube. Building on that, you will come to understand that your Why Statement will both serve as an inspiration as well as provide a clear and compelling image of your mission. "Why do you do what you do?"

Maintaining a strong "Why Statement" is important. It's what keeps your focus on the purpose of your business. It allows you to make clear decisions as well as set expectations about what people will receive from working for and with you.

A WHY Statement helps people to understand your true intentions. It also helps clarify whether you want a connection on an emotional or rational level. The simpler you make it, the easier it is for people to feel comfortable, and share their thoughts about your mission.

So, clearly define the real purpose of your storytelling and content creation. It is when you have a purpose, that you will be able to write with intention and make your content more impactful.

Here are 7 effective ways to write your why statement:

1. **Focus on your passions**: Think about the things that truly inspire and motivate you. What gets you out of bed in the morning? What do you enjoy doing, even when it's difficult? These passions can provide a starting point for your why statement.
2. **Consider your strengths**: Reflect on the skills and abilities that come naturally to you. What are you particularly good at? How do these strengths contribute to your personal sense of purpose?
3. **Think about your impact**: Consider how you want to make a difference in the world. What change do you want to see? How do you want to contribute to the greater good of mankind?
4. **Keep it simple**: Your why statement should be clear and concise. Avoid using jargon or

overly complicated language. Focus on a simple, straightforward expression of your purpose.

5. **Make it personal**: Your why statement should be a reflection of your unique perspective and experiences. Use language that feels authentic to who you are. This will help you stay connected to your why and maintain a sense of purpose over time.

6. **Be specific**: Avoid broad or generic statements that could apply to anyone. Instead, try to be as specific as possible about what drives you and what you hope to achieve. This will make your why statement more meaningful and memorable.

7. **Use storytelling**: One effective way to communicate your why statement is through storytelling. Share a personal anecdote or experience that highlights why you are passionate about your purpose. This can make your why statement more engaging and help others connect with your values and goals more easily.

By following these five tips, you can create a powerful and effective why statement that will guide you in your personal and professional life.

Storytelling guide - Define the why of your storytelling

Here are 5 tips to define the why of your storytelling:

1. **Identify the message you want to convey**: Before you begin writing your story, it's important to identify the message or lesson you want to convey to your audience. This will help you stay focused and ensure that your story has a clear purpose.
2. **Understand your audience**: Knowing your audience will help you tailor your story to their interests and needs. Ask yourself what they might be looking for in a story and what kind of message will resonate better with them.
3. **Consider your motivations**: Reflect on your motivations for telling this story. Are you trying to share a personal experience, raise awareness about a certain issue, or entertain your audience? Understanding your motivations will help you stay true to your story.
4. **Think about the larger context**: Consider the larger context in which your story is being told. What are the current events or issues that might be relevant to your story and your audience?
5. **Reflect on the impact of your story**: Think about the impact your story might have on your audience and the world at large. How do

you want your audience to feel after reading or hearing your story? And what kind of action do you want them to take?

These are important points to consider. By defining the why of your storytelling, you can ensure that your story has a clear purpose and message and that it will resonate with your audience. This will make your story more meaningful, engaging, and effective in delivering your intended message.

Your takeaway from chapter three

One of the key takeaways from this chapter is to be intentional about our storytelling. And one way is to define The Why Of Your Storytelling and stick to it.

Storytelling is more than just a skill it's a way of life. The art of storytelling is applied by telling stories with anecdotes, facts, and lessons to engage the listener and educate them about your perspective on a specific subject. It can be used to inspire and motivate people or just to share how you feel about something.

Doing all this takes a lot of time and that is why you need to be intentional about it. Why are you doing this, especially if you want to take it more seriously, like in a business environment as we shall consider later in this book series,

In this chapter of the book, we also learned that it is important to know what our values are and to create our "why" statement. All these are so that our storytelling has the ultimate results both for ourselves as the storytellers and the audience of our stories because no one has any time to waste these days.

In simpler terms, treat your storytelling as a serious business endeavor and it will pay you as one.

CHAPTER 4: THE 7 TYPES OF STORIES

The world of storytelling is vast and varied, but seven types of stories are essential to any narrative. From rags to riches, the quest to rebirth stories, discover the right type of stories that can captivate your audience and drive results for your business.

Master the art of storytelling with the seven types of stories that can easily resonate with any audience.

Welcome back to "**The Storytelling Mastery**". If you are a content creator and truly interested in storytelling, then you might want to know the type of storytelling to leverage in your content. This is what we are going to be learning in this chapter of the book.

As I have already alluded to in the previous book in this series, there are 7 types of stories, and they are as follows:

1. Rags to Riches,

2. Comedy,
3. Overcoming the Monster,
4. The Quest,
5. Voyage and Return,
6. Tragedy,
7. And rebirth.

Now, let's look at each of them more closely.

Rags to riches stories

The term "rags to riches" is often used in stories to denote a person who starts in poverty and eventually becomes wealthy in life.

In the story, a modest and moral but downtrodden character achieves a happy ending when his or her natural talents are discovered, or he or she has worked hard for years without appreciation.

So, in a rags-to-riches type of story, your character starts with nothing and goes on to become very successful. This is a common theme in literature and there are some examples of it in popular culture too.

If you are the movie type, here are 3 popular rags to riches films you might need to re-watch for better understanding:

➢ *Rocky - 1976*

Rocky is a drama/sports movie with over a million-dollar budget, and it was released in 1976. Rocky Balboa is a small-time boxer who gets a chance to fight the heavyweight champion of the world, Apollo Creed.

Rocky has his eyes on glory and only wants to earn respect by taking down what others have failed to do. This will not be easy but Sylvester Stallone, starring as Rocky Balboa will eventually become the champion.

➢ *Scarface - 1983*

Scarface is a 1983 Crime/Drama movie with some $66 million at the Box office. Here is the take: Tony Montana builds a powerful drug empire in Miami, but as his power grows, so do his ego and enemies.

He becomes paranoid and eventually destroys the only source of the money he has left.

➢ *The Pursuit Of Happyness - 2006*

The Pursuit Of Happyness is a 2006 drama movie, starring the legendary Will Smith as Chris with over $300 million sold at the Box office. Here is the takeaway: Chris' wife separated from him and that was a huge setback.

In addition to having his family fall apart, it also leaves him financially in a bad place. He has an unpaid internship and the custody of his son to take care of. But he finally makes it and his life turns around.

Rags to riches type of storytelling can be used in different places and genres of literature. Anyone with great skills that have the potential to succeed can use this approach in the "real world".

This includes people from a wide range of careers, including photographers, musicians, bloggers, digital entrepreneurs, and much more.

Content creators can use these stories to sell their products and services, by giving readers a sense of hope that they too can overcome their struggles.

For more about how to use stories in your content creation business, you need to see a later book in the series, "**The Storytelling Mastery**", where we shall talk about content entrepreneurship and everything about the business side of storytelling.

These types of stories also work well when used as social media posts or blog posts because they are more likely to get shared on social media and generate traffic back to your website.

Comedy stories

Comedy stories can be in the form of movies, books, or stage dramas. It is usually of light and humorous character with a happy or cheerful ending. Comedy stories are often about the happy endings of people who may have suffered misfortune in the past.

Comedy stories are unlike the more tragic stories found in some other genres of storytelling. Some key features of comedy are exaggerated physical characteristics and verbal humor which is often self-deprecating or poking fun at its subject matter.

David Khari Webber Chappelle, popularly known as Dave Chappelle is an American stand-up comedian and actor. He is best known for his satirical comedy sketch series, the "Chappelle's Show", which he starred in until quitting in the middle of production during the third season in 2005.

It was learned that Comedy Central offered him a whopping $50 million to do a third and fourth season of the show which Dave walked away from. How can you walk away from $50 million? Many did not understand.

While Chappelle did say in The Late Show with David Letterman that "Technically, I never quit", he was quoted as saying in another interview that "celebrities reaching the next height of their career often take large sums of money and end up going crazy."

Was Dave Chappelle actually protecting himself, or the popularity he has earned in the comedy empire? We might never know the whole truth. However, the message remains that if done correctly, you too, tapping into the power of comedy, can become a superstar.

As for how many years ago Dave Chappelle started his comedy career and has been honing his craft, he has this to say:

> *"I started when I was 14. I figured out that's what I wanted to do when I was 14. Even when I was six, I can remember people telling me, "You're gonna be a comedian," and all this stuff."*[12]

Studies show that there has been a recent rise in the comic and comedy industry, especially thanks to the age of the internet and portable digital devices, for recording and mastering digital content.

Do you like to create funny videos and post them to YouTube and other social media channels to make

---

[12] *Dave Chappelle - an American stand-up comedian and actor.*

people laugh? This can be one way for you to earn money from storytelling.

Comedy stories have been around as long as humans can tell stories, and they can be found in various cultures throughout history.

Apart from the already mentioned types of comedy stories such as movies or stage dramas, comedy can also exist as serialized television programming, such as sitcoms, animated cartoons, and much more.

Because comedy stories are a great way to make people laugh and make them feel good, these types of stories can be used in many ways to create marketing and educational content.

For example, they can be used as a form of entertainment in the workplace, or to help with your campaigns. Another popular type of storytelling is Overcoming the Monster stories. Let's find out more about it.

Overcoming the Monster stories

The Monster stories are a set of stories that are told primarily to teach children about the dangers of the world. This type of story has been told for generations, and many people still use it today. They are often told before bedtime to scare children into behaving well.

As a personal story, I have a son of 5 years, and each night before he goes to bed, he usually makes sure our contract of daily storytelling is respected. It doesn't matter if he has heard the story several times before. He just wants to hear stories.

What about you, do you usually hear some bedtime stories before you sleep? That is the type of story we are talking about here.

These days, however, we have a new set of monsters that need to be addressed: technology and social media.

Many parents feel as though they cannot keep up with their children's use of technology and social media, which is why they often resort to these old-fashioned methods of discipline or punishment to try and scare their children from using these devices too much.

Unlike other types of stories, Monster tales don't usually involve any random subplots to make it work. It is just good versus evil or hero vs villain.

There's one important point I want to mention here. The hero is usually an underdog in comparison to the villain, no matter what form they come, in monster stories, (political regime, corporate entity, or more.)

Here are some good examples of overcoming the monster stories:

1. Harry Potter series by J.K. Rowling - The series follows the story of a young boy, Harry Potter, who discovers that he is a wizard and must defeat the evil Lord Voldemort, who killed his parents and seeks to rule the wizarding world.
2. **Star Wars series** - The original trilogy features Luke Skywalker, who learns that he is a Jedi and must defeat the Galactic Empire, and Darth Vader, who killed his father and seeks to control the galaxy.
3. **The Hunger Games series by Suzanne Collins** - Set in a dystopian future, the story follows a young girl, Katniss Everdeen, who must survive the deadly Hunger Games, a televised competition where children from different districts fight to the death.
4. **The Lord of the Rings trilogy by J.R.R. Tolkien** - The story follows a hobbit named Frodo Baggins, who must journey to Mount Doom to destroy the One Ring, a powerful artifact that would give its wielder the power to rule over all of Middle-earth.
5. **The Matrix series** - The story follows a young man named Neo, who discovers that his reality is a simulated world created by

machines, and must fight to free humanity from their control.

6. **The Chronicles of Narnia series by C.S. Lewis** - The series follows a group of children who enter the magical world of Narnia and must fight against the evil witch, Jadis, who seeks to rule over the land and bring eternal winter.

7. **Wonder Woman** - The character of Wonder Woman, created by William Moulton Marston, is a classic "overcoming the monster" story. As an Amazon princess, she battles against powerful villains and evil forces, using her strength, wisdom, and compassion to save the world from destruction.

These stories all follow the pattern of the "overcoming the monster" archetype, where the protagonist faces a powerful and often evil force that threatens their world and must overcome it through strength, courage, and determination.

In overcoming the monster stories, the protagonist goes through adversity with perseverance but often overcomes a powerful, threatening force. The protagonist has an internal conflict, which is their internal struggle with themselves and what they want to do versus what they need to do.

The external conflict is what is going on outside of them - like their family, friends, work, or school. Those conflicts make it hard for them to focus on their goals. The story has a happy ending when the protagonist manages to overcome all of these obstacles and overcomes the monster in some way.

Want to learn more about conflicts in storytelling, check out the second book in the (Storytelling Series for African Diaspora: Beginners' Guide for Small Businesses & Content Creators). Chapter 4 of the book dealt exhaustively with that.

Overcoming the monster stories is a great way to break the ice and get your audience hooked on your content. Not only do they have a dramatic story, but they also have an element of surprise.

The Quest stories

Do you remember the main characters in your favorite fairytale and how they often face obstacles to gain new knowledge, skills, and experiences? They usually get a helping hand along the way and end up living happily ever after.

A quest is a heroic journey, typically one to recover something or to prove oneself. In medieval Roman, the term "quests" refers to chivalric adventures. These were fantastic stories about, often a chivalric knight-errant portrayed as having heroic qualities, who goes on a quest.

The protagonist of a quest story typically meets with and overcomes a series of obstacles, returning in the end with either a prize or at least some news of success.

Quest stories are a popular genre in literature and there are certain elements to be addressed for the quest to succeed.

There needs to be a clear goal and a clear antagonist, which can be something or someone. Some good examples of quest stories are as follows:

1. **The Hobbit by J.R.R. Tolkien** - The story follows the hobbit, Bilbo Baggins, on a journey to reclaim the lost treasure of the dwarves from the dragon Smaug.
2. **The Odyssey by Homer** - The ancient Greek epic poem tells the story of Odysseus, who embarks on a long journey back home after the Trojan War.
3. **The Lion, The Witch, and The Wardrobe by C.S. Lewis** - The first book in The Chronicles of Narnia series follows four siblings who journey to the magical land of Narnia to fulfill their destiny and help Aslan defeat the White Witch.
4. **Indiana Jones series** - The series follows the adventures of archaeologist Indiana Jones, who goes on quests to find lost artifacts and protect them from dangerous groups.

5. **The Lord of the Rings trilogy by J.R.R. Tolkien** - The story follows Frodo and his companions as they journey to Mount Doom to destroy the One Ring and defeat the evil forces of Sauron.
6. **The Alchemist by Paulo Coelho** - The story follows a shepherd boy named Santiago on a quest to find a treasure he saw in his dreams, encountering various obstacles and learning important life lessons along the way.
7. **The Wizard of Oz by L. Frank Baum** - The story follows Dorothy and her dog Toto on a quest to find the Wizard of Oz and return home to Kansas, meeting strange and interesting characters along the way.

These stories all follow the pattern of "the Quest" archetype, where the protagonist goes on a journey or adventure to achieve a specific goal, facing challenges and obstacles along the way.

Voyage and return stories

The Voyage and Return type of storytelling is a tale that follows a general arc. Just as in the Hero's Journey, the protagonist ventures forth into the unknown, and at first, the world of the unknown is fascinating and new.

However, as the hero explores it more thoroughly, he or she realizes that this new world is not all that it seems at first glance.

For a good voyage and return story, the protagonist usually encounters obstacles along the way, and upon finally returning home, they are gifted with new knowledge or insight as to how to make their life better.

Some good examples of these types of stories are:

- The Wonderful Wizard of Oz,
- Alice's Adventures in Wonderland,
- Through the Looking Glass,
- Gone with the Wind,

Many content marketers of today are using these stories to create a narrative around their products or services and much more. One of the great things about this type of story is that it provides stories with opportunities for marketers to show how their product or service can help consumers achieve their goals.

There is another important and popular type of story and they are called a tragedy. Let's look at it.

Tragedy type of stories

Sometimes the best way to explore life is through the lens of death and setbacks. Tragedy in literature can teach us lessons about life, love, and human nature. It can also provoke deep and powerful emotions that might not be as accessible in other genres of storytelling.

Hamlet, for example, has remained the most popular and well-known of all of Shakespeare's plays. It is considered to be one of the most influential tragedies in English literature, as well as one of the author's most powerful pieces.

Some other examples of Tragedies include Romeo and Juliet.

In the story of Romeo and Juliet, the two young lovers meet, and fall in love, but because of their families' age-old feud, they are going to face a terrible fate. Juliet's cousin, Tybalt kills Romeo's friend Mercutio, and that leads to even more questions and challenges for Romeo and Juliet.

As you already know, tragedies are stories that are sad, depressing, or tragic. It is used in advertising and marketing to create an emotional appeal.

The best way to use a tragic story in content marketing is to combine it with an inspirational message. This will make the audience feel empowered and hopeful instead of sad or depressed.

Here are 6 more examples of popular tragedy stories to learn from:

1. **The Great Gatsby by F. Scott Fitzgerald** - The novel follows the tragic story of Jay Gatsby, a wealthy man who becomes obsessed with winning back his lost love, Daisy Buchanan.
2. **Death of a Salesman by Arthur Miller** - The play tells the story of an aging salesman named Willy Loman, whose life spirals out of control as he struggles to achieve the American Dream.
3. **Hamlet by William Shakespeare** - The play follows the story of Prince Hamlet, who seeks revenge for his father's murder but ultimately meets a tragic end.
4. **A Streetcar Named Desire by Tennessee Williams** - The play tells the story of Blanche DuBois, a fading Southern belle who struggles to adapt to a changing world and ultimately meets a tragic fate.
5. **Oedipus Rex by Sophocles** - The ancient Greek play tells the story of Oedipus, a king who unknowingly fulfills a prophecy that he will kill his father and marry his mother, leading to his downfall.

6. **One Hundred Years of Solitude by Gabriel Garcia Marquez** - The novel follows the Buendia family through several generations in the fictional town of Macondo, as they experience a range of tragedies and struggles to find meaning and purpose in life.

These stories all follow the pattern of the "Tragedy" archetype of storytelling, where the protagonist faces a downfall or an unfortunate ending due to their flaws, mistakes, or external forces beyond their control.

Rebirth stories

Rebirth storytelling is another important type of narrative that is used to convey a story through the use of birth, death, and rebirth. It can be used in any medium to convey a powerful message to the audience.

Charles Dickens's A Christmas Carol is a well-known story of rebirth. Other stories where the protagonist experiences a change after realizing the error of their ways include:

- The Secret Garden,
- Beauty and the Beast,
- And Groundhog Day in a long list of others.

Rebirth storytelling is not just about death and resurrection. It's also about the process of growth, transformation, and renewal. This again can be a great type of story to tell in a business environment.

The power of rebirth storytelling lies in its ability to make the audience feel like they are part of the story. It taps into their emotions and this is what makes it so powerful, especially for marketing purposes.

As you can see, there are different types of stories you can explore for your content creation and satisfy the needs of your audience. So, pick the one that can work better for you and run with it.

Storytelling guide - The seven types of stories

The seven types of stories, also known as the seven basic plots can be used in a business setting to help convey a message or make a point in a more engaging and relatable way. Here are a few examples of how you can use them:

1. Use Overcoming the Monster story to demonstrate how your company successfully overcame a major challenge or obstacle.
2. Use the Rags to Riches story to show how your company has grown and evolved.
3. Use The Quest story to demonstrate your company's mission and purpose.

4. Use the Voyage and Return story to describe the journey of a customer or employee who has used your product or service.
5. Use the Comedy story to lighten the mood and create a more positive and engaging message.
6. Use the Tragedy story to demonstrate the importance of your product or service in preventing a negative outcome.
7. Use the Rebirth story to describe a major change or transformation that your company has undergone.

Overall, using these types of stories can help to make your message more relatable, engaging, and memorable for your audience, whether it's potential customers, employees, or investors.

Your Takeaway from Chapter Four

The topic discussed in this chapter, "The Seven Types Of Stories" is one you cannot ignore when studying the basics of storytelling because it helps you to understand the different stories out there and what makes one different from the other.

Christopher Booker's book The Seven Basic Plots: Why We Tell Stories was the first to identify the seven basic story types we talked about in this chapter. In his book, Booker argues that any story can be boiled down to one of these types. You can consider checking out the book to learn more.

Learning about the seven basic types of stories in this chapter helps you understand that stories are more like a lot of people. They wear different clothes and live in different places. Some are happy, and some are sad. And many reappear across eras and cultures - such as "voyage and return" or "hero's journey" - which is what makes them so powerful.

Knowing the seven basic plots and how they are different means you can now use similar story plots in your way and with your message. The next chapter will be about telling a memorable story. So, get ready for that.

CHAPTER 5: TELLING A MEMORABLE STORY

As humans, we are wired to remember stories. From ancient times when our ancestors huddled around the fire to share tales of their heroic hunts, to the present day when people binge-watch entire series on streaming platforms, stories have always captivated us.

The difference between a forgettable story and a memorable one lies in the way it is told. If one wants to leave a lasting impression on their audience, whether it's a group of friends or a boardroom full of executives, one needs to know how to tell a memorable story.

Congratulations and welcome to the last chapter of the book, How To Tell Your Personal Story: The Essential Guide To Memorable Storytelling. This is book three in "**The Storytelling Mastery**".

This chapter of the book will pay attention to the key elements of storytelling, and help you explore some practical tips on how to make stories more engaging and unforgettable to your audience.

Do you know how to tell a memorable story? Now, think about the following for a moment: up until a few years ago, the term "Black Lives Matter" did not enter your memory. The Black Lives Matter (BLM) movement which started on July 13, 2013, following the death of George Floyd is a powerful example of a memorable story.

The BLM story was rooted in deep-seated emotional experiences and focuses on the systemic issues of racial inequality and police brutality faced by the African diaspora community in the United States and other parts of Western countries. It highlights universal themes of justice, equality, and human rights, which resonate with people from all backgrounds.

The BLM story has been told through various forms of media, including protests, social media, and traditional news outlets. This has allowed the movement to reach a wider audience and evoke a powerful emotional response. The vivid language used to describe the experiences of individuals in the African diaspora community has helped bring the story to life and connect with people on a deeper level.

Do you know what makes a memorable story and how it can impact your audience in terms of better connection?

> "The best storytellers look to their own memories and life experiences for ways to illustrate their message. What events in your life make you believe in the idea you are trying to share?"[13]

That was from the article, How to Tell a Great Story by Carolyn O'Hara, a contributor to the Harvard Business Review.

The advice from Carolyn is to start with a message, saying that "every storytelling exercise should begin by asking: Who is my audience and what is the message I want to share with them?" Now is the time to answer the question: what is a memorable story?

What is a memorable story?

A memorable story is a story that stays with you long after you have heard it, one that you can easily recall and retell. It has elements that make it unique, engaging, and impactful. Below are some qualities of a memorable story. Now as you go through these

---

[13] How to Tell a Great Story - Hbr.org.

qualities, consider the Black Lives Matter story I referenced at the beginning of this chapter:

1. **Emotional resonance**: A memorable story resonates with the audience on an emotional level, evoking feelings of empathy, excitement, sadness, or joy.
2. **Clear structure**: A memorable story has a clear beginning, middle, and end that is easy to follow and understand.
3. **Relatable characters**: A memorable story has well-developed characters that the audience can relate to and care about.
4. **Unique premise**: A memorable story has a unique and interesting premise that sets it apart from other stories and captures the audience's attention.
5. **Meaningful message**: A memorable story has a deeper meaning or message that stays with the audience long after the story has ended.
6. **Impactful ending**: A memorable story has a satisfying and impactful ending that leaves a lasting impression on the audience.

Want your story to be memorable to your audience? Make sure you observe the qualities mentioned above. An example of a memorable story is "The Shawshank Redemption." The story has relatable characters, a clear structure, and a unique premise that sets it apart from other stories. The emotional resonance of the story, combined with its meaningful message, makes it a story that stays with the audience long after it has ended.

Another example is "To Kill a Mockingbird." The story has well-developed characters, a clear structure, and a unique premise that captivates the audience. The impactful ending, combined with the meaningful message about justice and morality, makes it a memorable story that has been beloved for generations.

A memorable story has a lasting impact on its audience in their memory, long after they have heard it. By incorporating emotional resonance, clear structure, relatable characters, a unique premise, a meaningful message, and an impactful ending, you can create a story that will be remembered for years to come.

Here are some strategies to employ if want your story to be truly memorable to your audience:

Make your stories emotionally rich

Emotions play a critical role in storytelling because they are what makes a story memorable. When a story resonates emotionally with an audience, it sticks with them long after they have finished reading or listening to it. An emotionally rich story will get people to take action all the time and that is why it always works.

Give your audience something to feel and they will feel it. Also from the point of view of anthropology, all humans are essentially tribal species. If you can rightly appeal to their emotion, you can almost be guaranteed to have them on your side.

There is another way to look at it. Now, picture the African diaspora community as a drum circle, where each individual is a unique drum with their own rhythm and story to tell. When these drums come together, they create a rich and powerful sound, representing the strength and unity of the community. Emotional storytelling serves as the heartbeat of the drum circle, connecting each drum and weaving their stories into a collective rhythm that evokes shared emotions and a sense of belonging.

The power of emotional storytelling in the African diaspora community is what creates a deep and unforgettable rhythm, one that transcends borders and unites the community in a harmonious bond. So, as a storyteller, you need to leverage this power to your favor.

In an interesting article: How to Craft Emotionally Complex Characters, the writer threw some questions to the readers:

"If I were to ask who you are, you'd likely answer by sharing the labels you feel define your identity, which may include your profession, racial or ethnic background, political or religious affiliations, who you are in relation to your loved ones, what hobbies and interests you enjoy, and so on."[14]

As readers, said the article, we carry this same tendency to identify, label, and categorize our relationship with storytelling, particularly in the way we view characters. Stories are a powerful instrument to connect with people at an emotional level. Now, here are some tips to help you tap into your audience's emotions so you can make better connections:

1. **Identify your audience's emotional state**: Before you begin, think about what emotions your audience is likely feeling. Are they sad, happy, frustrated, angry, or hopeful? Understanding their emotional state will help you craft a story that resonates with them.
2. **Use personal experiences**: Sharing personal experiences that evoke strong emotions is a great way to connect with your

---

[14] *How to Craft Emotionally Complex Characters - Well-storied.com.*

audience. People relate to stories that are authentic and come from the heart.

3. **Use descriptive language**: The words you choose to use in your story can either enhance or detract from the emotional impact of your story. Use descriptive language to paint a vivid picture of the events and emotions you want to convey.

4. **Vary the pace**: Changing the pace of your story can create tension and heighten emotions. Slow the pace when describing a particularly emotional moment to give your audience time to process what they are feeling.

5. **Use sensory details**: Involving multiple senses in your storytelling helps to create a more immersive experience for your audience. Use descriptive language to bring sights, sounds, smells, and textures to life so you can better tap into their emotion.

By incorporating these actionable tips, you can perfectly tap into your audience's emotions and craft a memorable story that resonates with them.

Understanding the art of story structure

The structure of a story is essential to making it engaging and memorable. A well-structured story has a clear beginning, middle, and end that keeps the audience invested and interested in the outcome. If you want to learn more about story structure, you might need to check out Storytelling Basics, the first book in this 5-part book series. We dedicated chapter 4 of that book to talk about story structure.

By understanding the art of story structure, you can create an easily impactful story to leverage in your small business or content creation. Now, here are some tips to help you craft a more compelling narrative:

1. **Start with a strong opening:** The opening of a story is like a first impression. It sets the tone and establishes the narrative. Make sure your opening is engaging and immediately draws the audience into the narration.
2. **Develop rising action:** The rising action is part of the story that builds tension and keeps the audience engaged. It is often where the protagonist faces obstacles and struggles to achieve their goal.
3. **Build to a climax:** The climax is the peak of the story, the moment of greatest tension or conflict. It is the turning point in the narrative and often determines the outcome of the story.
4. **Provide good resolution:** The resolution is the conclusion of the story, where loose ends are tied up and the audience finds out what happens to the characters. It should provide

a satisfying conclusion that leaves a lasting impression on your audience.

One good example of a well-structured story is "The Wizard of Oz." The opening line introduces the protagonist and sets the stage for Dorothy's journey. The rising action follows her as she faces obstacles and meets new characters along the way.

The climax is the moment she finally reaches the wizard and must confront him to achieve her goal. The resolution ties up the loose ends and brings the story to a satisfying conclusion.

Another example is "The Pursuit of Happyness". The opening of the story introduces the protagonist, a struggling salesman, and sets the stage for his journey. The rising action follows him as he faces numerous obstacles and struggles to provide for his family.

The climax is the moment he finally lands a job interview that could change his life. The resolution ties up the loose ends and provides a satisfying conclusion that leaves a lasting impression on the audience.

Want to leave a lasting impression on your audience, consider the tips above and learn the art of story structure. Mastering the art of story structure, you can comfortably craft a compelling narrative that keeps your audience engaged and invested in your story from beginning to end. That is what every storyteller must learn how to do.

Leverage your personal story to connect more

Telling your personal story can be a powerful way to connect with your audience. By sharing your experiences and emotions, you can create a deeper level of intimacy and understanding with your audience.

Now, let me create a little story, and let's see what you can get out of it:

Once upon a time, there was a content creator. Let's call him Adudu, which means shadow in the Esan language of Nigeria. For years, Adudu struggled to connect with his audience. He felt like his content was falling flat and that his audience wasn't fully engaged. Adudu felt lost and didn't know what to do.

One day, a wise mentor told him about the power of storytelling. The mentor explained that by sharing a personal story, Adudu could build a deeper connection with his audience.

Adudu was skeptical at first but eventually decided to give it a try. He started by being authentic and sharing his experiences, struggles, and triumphs along the way. He also focused on emotions, highlighting universal themes, and using vivid language to bring his content creation story to life.

As Adudu continued to practice and refine his storytelling skills, he noticed a change in his audience's engagement. His audience was now more invested in his content, and then he felt like he had finally found a way to connect with his audience on a deeper level.

Adudu continued to share his story and inspire others to do the same. Soon he became known for his powerful and meaningful storytelling, and his audience continued to grow. Now Adudu learned that by leveraging his personal story, he could build a lasting connection with his audience and make a meaningful impact with his storytelling.

This is only to get you thinking and I want to believe you get the point about the importance of leveraging your personal story to connect with your audience.

For example, when TEDx speaker Simon Sinek spoke about his struggles with depression and how it affected his life and work, he was able to connect with his audience on a personal level and inspire them with his message of hope. By sharing his personal story, he was able to build a deeper connection with his audience and leave a lasting impact on them.

Another example is Oprah Winfrey, who has used her personal story to connect with her audience and build a media empire. Do not say it cannot be done in your case because you can if you want. We all have stories to share as I keep repeating in my podcast (Obehi Podcast). By sharing her journey from poverty to success, Oprah Winfrey has inspired millions of people and created a strong emotional connection with her audience.

Telling your personal story can be a powerful way to connect with your audience and leave a lasting impact.

Here are some ways telling your personal story can help you connect with your audience. I encourage you to try out these tips in your stories:

1. **Be authentic**: The most powerful personal stories are ones that are authentic and honest. Be vulnerable and open up about your experiences, struggles, and triumphs. Your audience will appreciate the honesty and will be able to connect with you on a deeper level.
2. **Focus on emotions**: Your personal story should evoke emotions in your audience. Emphasize the emotions you experienced and try to bring the audience along on that journey with you.
3. **Highlight universal themes**: Try to find universal themes in your personal story that

are relevant to your audience. For example, everyone can relate to overcoming obstacles, finding purpose, or following their passions. By highlighting these universal themes, your story will have a wider appeal and resonate with more people.

4. **Use vivid language**: To be more impactful with your personal stories, use descriptive language to bring your story to life. The more vivid your descriptions, the more your audience will be able to see and feel what you experienced.

5. **Find a balance between vulnerability and professionalism**: Be careful not to overshare in a way that might be seen as unprofessional. Find a balance between being vulnerable and sharing your story, and being mindful of the image you want to present to your audience.

6. **Practice**: Like any skill, storytelling takes practice. Rehearse your story and refine it until it flows naturally and hits all the key points you want to convey.

Pay attention to these helpful tips and apply them in your storytelling. Do it well and you can effectively leverage your personal story to connect with your audience and build a deeper, more meaningful relationship with them.

Storytelling guide – Tell a memorable story

Memorable stories are the only type of stories you should tell so you can always leave a good impression on the minds of your audience. Here are 4 effective ways to tell a memorable story:

1. **Start with Emotion**: Emotions are a powerful tool in storytelling and can help to engage your audience and make your story memorable. Tap into your own emotions or those of your characters to add depth and meaning to your story.
2. **Create a Strong Narrative Arc**: A strong narrative arc is a crucial element in making a story memorable. Your story should have a clear beginning, middle, and end, and each part should build on the previous one to create a compelling journey.
3. **Practice and Refine**: Like any skill, storytelling takes practice to perfect. Take the time to refine your story and make sure it flows naturally. Pay attention to pacing, tone, and other elements that can impact the overall effectiveness of your story.
4. **Make It Visual**: Visual storytelling is a powerful tool to help make your story more memorable. Whether it's through illustrations, images, or videos, visual storytelling can help

bring your story to life and keep your audience engaged.

Your takeaway from Chapter Five

If you want to be truly connected to your audience, you need to tell memorable stories. That has been the focus of this chapter of the book. A memorable story is a story that stays with you long after you have heard it, one that you can easily recall and retell. It has elements that make it unique, engaging, and impactful.

We learned that for a story to leave a lasting impression, it must contain an element of tension and uniqueness at its core. And this can be done by leveraging the different helpful tips that were shared in different parts of this chapter. I hope that you have paid attention to them and will apply them as you go about creating your memorable stories.

Some of the highlights of the chapter were what are memorable stories, how to make your stories emotionally rich, how to understand the art of story structure, and how to leverage your personal story to connect more.

All these are the instruments to drive home the point about creating a memorable story and I want to believe we have done so.

CONCLUSION

Congratulations and thanks for reading to the end of this book. As you close the pages of this book, you will be armed with the tools and skills you need to turn your personal story into a captivating narrative.

You now know how to identify the themes that drive your story, how to develop dynamic characters, and create moments of tension that will keep your audience engaged. All these are the hallmarks of good storytelling and that is what you need to do for your audience.

But the most important lesson of all is that storytelling is not just about entertaining others, it's about empowering yourself. By sharing your experiences through the art of storytelling, you will not only connect with others, but you will also gain a deeper understanding of yourself and your own life journey.

In the pages of this book, you have learned the key elements of storytelling, from Knowing Your Personal Story and Defining the Why of Your Storytelling to the all-important how to tell a memorable story. You don't want to underestimate any of these.

You have explored techniques for developing dynamic characters, creating moments of tension, and bringing your stories to life through vivid descriptions and dialogue. You have also discovered the power of theme, and how to use it to drive your narrative forward and I really wish you can take advantage of that.

Another thing we learned in this chapter of the book is the importance of authenticity and how to stay true to yourself as you craft your stories. And now, as you step away from this book. I am confident that you are ready to start sharing your personal stories with the world.

Remember, storytelling is not just about regaling others with your experiences, it's also a tool for self-expression and self-discovery. So go forth, share your story, and inspire others with the power of your own experiences.

ABOUT THE AUTHOR

My name is Obehi Ewanfoh. I am originally from Nigeria and I live in Verona, Italy with my family. I am a full-time content creator and I love to create valuable content to inform and educate my audience.

I am the host of the Obehi Podcast where we strongly believe that everyone has a story to share. By everyone, I mean everyone and that includes you.

Upon arriving in Italy in August of 2004, I found myself asking such questions as:

- Who were the first Africans in the city of Verona where I have lived since then?
- What have been their experiences away from their homeland?
- As an immigrant, new to the Northern Italy city of Verona, how could I learn from them?

I could not find any book to read and some of the information I could find here and there was not satisfactory to me, so I decided to start asking more questions and talking to different people with the idea of writing the first book of the African experience in the city.

The research would take more than five years and result in more than two books (*The Journey—Africans In Verona* and *The Colour Of Our Children*), in addition to some video documentaries, which were screened in different schools and cultural centers across Northern Italy.

Even then I was still not fully satisfied because there were no real solutions to the complains I heard from people for more than five years, and I was not sure if I had made any real contributions by asking those questions.

A little later, exactly on April the 7th 2019, it occurred to me like a deeper message. I was hospitalized then and I was thinking a lot about this project I have been working on for a long time.

This was when I realized that I really needed to do this. Thinking back to when I was much younger in my hometown of Uromi, Nigeria, and the different books I have written, both published and unpublished.

It came to make sense to me, then, that I was searching for myself, my way of contributing to other people and living a life that truly makes sense to me.

I have since come to appreciate this opportunity of service, of helping other people to find what they truly love and to make their contributions, especially through storytelling and content creation.

Storytelling, you will understand in this book on Storytelling Basics, is a powerful instrument to leverage either for personal use or business purposes. This is why the book series: **The Storytelling Mastery: How To Elevate Your Business and Build Personal Influence with The Power Of Storytelling** was created. It is designed to help you leverage the power of storytelling so you can stand out from the crowd and earn more.

My ultimate mission, through content creation, is to help people, particularly those within the African diaspora community, to transform their human potential into capital so they can better serve themselves and the society they live in.

If you found any value in this book, then it means my journey has somehow been a success. Thank you again for reading,

Obehi Ewanfoh.